We'll Always Have This

Natasha Kyler

BookLeaf Publishing

We'll Always Have This © 2021 Natasha Kyler

Presentation by *BookLeaf Publishing*

Web: www.bookleafpub.com

E-mail: info@bookleafpub.com

ISBN - 9789358366617

First edition 2021

For all the people that aren't around to see
how greatly they impacted my life.

Acknowledgement

A special thanks to Tyra for motivating me when I needed it most. She helped me focus on what was important and meeting deadlines. Niyah for helping me choose my last poem and assuring me that it went with my theme. I must thank Brooklyn, Demi, and Kirah for not only encouraging my participation in this challenge but also giving me ideas from themes to lines and associations. To Annette, Bri, and Dori for believing in my babbles with no substance.

1.

All of a sudden
You became a chore
Rather than my friend.

Dread replaced the butterflies
And boredom replaced interest.
Anything could be better than this.

Complacent in avoidance,
Finding everything annoying,
This can't be healthy.

Guilt-ridden but unsure why
This feeling will go away in time
Just please, go back to being my friend.

2.

It's always the same
Words spoken at me
Like a broken record
Never to me, never personal
Like an infomercial
I sit through the repetition
Wishing for something more
Something original
Just another day with
Nothing new, nothing special
- have you always been this predictable?

3.

Acknowledging its presence
Makes it real
And I'd rather play pretend
As long as I can.

Like a secret
It lives in my head
But I refuse to make sense of it
Because once I do
There will be no hope left.

- they say ignorance is bliss

4.

The trees are starting to die
Revealing beautiful scenery
Reminding me of our history
As our love dwindles out.

Sweaters shielding
Out the cold
Like defensiveness
Hiding our problems.

The fading
Of orange to brown,
Of enthusiasm to isolation,
We're like the changing of seasons.

5.

Hold on to the present
Release the past.
Relish our good moments
And talk out our bad ones.

I spend my time reminding myself
To do these things.
I'm in my head as if
We've come to a crossroads.
But this fog will lift
And it'll all be worth it.

6.

I have such a weakness for you,
You can always find your way
Back to my heart.
No matter how this turns out
I'll always let you be
The death of me.

7.

I thought I was overthinking
But it's becoming evident
You see what I see
And feel what I feel.

Now you're say all the things
You think I want to hear
In an attempt to
Close the distance between us.

You know what it takes
To get back into my heart
But what you don't know
Is that you never really left.

8.

Just as I begin to walk away
You pull me back in
Like a game of cat and mouse
Where the roles are ever-changing
And we can't seem to accept
The hand that fate has dealt us.

We search for something within each
other
The people we used to be or
The memories we fell for or
Maybe a reason but
Eventually I will tire of looking for
reasons
To stay, to choose your happiness over
mine.

9.

You used to gaze upon me as if
My soul was your deepest desire.
Now you look at me slightly out of focus,
Blurring the version of me that truly exists
And your idea of me.

You don't listen to me as if
I speak a foreign language,
You hear only what you want
And label the rest gibberish.

The distance between us grows farther,
Galaxies apart when we used to be on the
same planet.
Do either of us care?
Do we even stand a chance of going back
to how it was?

10.

Hopeless romantic lost to comfort
Can you fall once more
In love with us
And in lust with life?

Dreams ruined by fear of love
Can you ever be as pretty as before
Even if we tremble
At the very thought of you?

Hearts that were crushed
Will you forgive us
For the atrocities we committed
In our state of commitment?

Love from the past
It's impossible to be you
But we try our best to emulate
What we used to have.

11.

The puzzle was never missing a piece
We were putting together the wrong
picture
Making everything more difficult than
necessary
Rather than accepting our faults
And fixing the problem.

We got too ahead of ourselves
Thinking we could solve it
Individually, without any help
Forgetting we are stronger when we
collaborate.
Now it's too late for such epiphanies.

12.

These lips aren't the same ones that loved
me so sweetly
They're tainted with the bitterness that
comes from deceit

Yet I still want you to say it again
So my mind can rest
And we can put it behind us.

Sell me your lies
So that we can pretend
That everything is fine.

13.

I knew when
I didn't recognize you anymore
In my memories
In my writing
In my bed

I knew when
You felt 300 miles away
But you were only
Across the table

I knew when
The twinkle in your eye died
The smile I adored became rarer
The laughter turned to silence

I knew because I felt the same way too

14.

Is it strange that
I long to be engulfed by the
Anger that once consumed me
Yet I'm tired of resenting you
When its equally my fault.
Maybe I'm just tired
Of being angry at myself.
Maybe I'm just looking
For someone to blame
And the only options
Are me and you.

15.

Constellation of sadness
That wished to never be seen
Now on display for all.

If it's hidden, it's not real
Was the lie
Consuming its thoughts.

Its brightness dims,
In desperate need of an eclipse to
Overshadow these emotions

And hide the pain
The stars so desperately
Tried to erase.

16.

I still type out full text to you
Wanting to tell you about my day or
Something random that you'd appreciate
Then I remember you don't care anymore.
And it breaks my heart to
Find myself wishing we never met
When you act like a stranger in the cafe
Because there are a million things to say
But all you do is walk away.

17.

I was grateful to love you
To experience you
And have proof that I lived

You were a gentle touch
Breaking through my cement barrier,
Equipped with all the tools
Necessary to break me down.

But I'm more grateful to lose you
To have proof that I learned
You were part of a lesson
And now you've fulfilled your role.

18.

Love is a cycle
Fall in, get comfy
Get bored, fall out.

We look for permanence
And receive temporary.

Love is delusional
You have to feel it
Then you know it's real.

It distorts time and reality
But fills you with happiness.

19.

As we go our separate ways,
So many memories for you to take like

Every place you ever held me
Like where we sat in the rain.

Every show we ever binged
In a weekend, not remembering half of it.

Every lie we ever spoke
Especially "I love you" towards the end.

20.

Intuitively, we let go of each other
Long before we ever realized.
Like a snake shedding its skin
Wrapped in a cocoon of false security,
We became afraid of leaving the
And widening our horizons beyond the
Landscape directly in front of us
Like a crutch,
I'll be able to go on without you but
It will be painful and uncomfortable.
- growing pains

www.ingramcontent.com/pod-product-compliance
Lightning Source LLC
Chambersburg PA
CBHW071250140726
47996CB00007B/2824